ATLANTIC OCEAN

2 O Saragossa

1 Fuendetodos O

3 Madrid ☆

SPAIN

SPANISH OLIVES

PORTUGAL

5 Cádiz

6. FRANCE

Bordeaux

Parma

SPAIN

ITALY

Rome

4

MEDITERRANEAN SEA

MOROCCO

TIMELINE OF FRANCISCO GOYA'S LIFE

1746 Francisco is born in Fuendetodos, Spain.

1750s The Goya family moves to Saragossa. Francisco begins school and starts to show a talent for art.

1763 Francisco moves to Spain's capital, Madrid.

1770 Francisco Goya travels to Italy. He studies the works of master artists from the past, and enters an art show where he wins a second-place prize.

1771 Goya returns to Spain. He begins doing some religious paintings, as well as scenes of everyday Spanish life to be used as designs for making tapestries.

1773 Goya marries Josefa Bayeu.

1776-1788 Goya's tapestry-design paintings start getting noticed. He is soon asked to do portraits for important people, including the Spanish king and his family.

THIS WAY

1789 King Charles IV appoints Goya court painter.

1793 Francisco spends time in Cádiz while recovering from a mysterious disease. After his recovery, some of his paintings take on a surprising new look.

1808 When the French army invades Spain, Francisco Goya sees horrible events happening all around him. He creates some of his greatest works showing the horrors of war.

1819 Goya buys a large country home near Madrid. He paints terrifying pictures on the walls of his house for his own enjoyment.

1824 Francisco Goya retires to the French city of Bordeaux. He concentrates more on miniature paintings, drawings, and prints.

1828 Goya dies at his home in Bordeaux at the age of eighty-two.

UP HERE

GETTING TO KNOW THE WORLD'S GREATEST ARTISTS

FRANCISCO
GOYA

WRITTEN AND ILLUSTRATED BY MIKE VENEZIA

CONSULTANT SARA MOLLMAN UNDERHILL

CHILDREN'S PRESS®

An Imprint of Scholastic Inc.

Cover: *Witches' scene or Scene of an exorcism. Escena de brujas
o Escena de exorcismo.* 1797/98. Oil on canvas, 45 x 32 cm.
Museo Lazaro Galdiano-Coleccion, Madrid, Spain/Album/Art
Resource, NY

Library of Congress Cataloging-in-Publication Data

Names: Venezia, Mike, author, illustrator.
Title: Francisco Goya / Written and illustrated by Mike Venezia.
Description: Revised Edition. | New York : Childrens Press, 2016. | Series:
    Getting to know the world's greatest artists | Includes bibliographical
    references and index.
Identifiers: LCCN 2015037160| ISBN 9780531216675 (library binding : alk.
    paper) | ISBN 9780531221068 (pbk. : alk. paper)
Subjects: LCSH: Goya, Francisco, 1746-1828–Juvenile literature. |
    Painters–Spain–Biography–Juvenile literature.
Classification: LCC ND813.G7 V4 2016 | DDC 759.6–dc23 LC record available
at http://lccn.loc.gov/2015037160

SCHOLASTIC, CHILDREN'S PRESS, and associated logos are trademarks and/or
registered trademarks of Scholastic Inc.

1 2 3 4 5 6 7 8 9 10 R 25 24 23 22 21 20 19 18 17 16

Self-Portrait. 1815. Oil on canvas, 18 x 13¾ inches.
Prado, Madrid. Bridgeman Art Library/SuperStock

Francisco Goya was born in
Fuendetodos, Spain, in 1746. He
was one of Spain's greatest artists
and discovered new ways of painting
that led to the exciting world of
modern art.

The Family of the Duke of Osuna. 1788. Oil on canvas, 88⅝ x 67⅜ inches.
Prado, Madrid. Scala/Art Resource, NY

During his life, Goya painted
portraits of the wealthy people in
Spain's royal court. Dukes, duchesses,
kings, and queens paid Goya to make
paintings of them.

The Colossus. 1811. Oil on canvas, 45¾ x 41⅜ inches.
Prado, Madrid. Bridgeman Art Library/SuperStock

Sometimes Goya made paintings just for himself. He painted things that interested him, and things that came from his mysterious and secret thoughts.

   While Francisco Goya was growing
up, Spain was a very poor country.
The Spanish king was spending most
of Spain's money on wars, and the
rest went to the king's greedy,

rich friends. Almost everyone else
was very poor.

Cities didn't have garbage pickup
or street lights or police departments.
Roads were rocky and bumpy and
bandits were all over the place!

Regina Martirum. (portion) 1780-81. Cupola fresco.
Basilica del Pilar, Zaragoza. Oronoz, Madrid

When Goya was about 12 years old, his mother and father decided to leave the dusty town of Fuendetodos, and move to the busy city of Saragossa. It was an important move for Francisco Goya.

The city of Saragossa had churches

that were filled with beautiful
paintings and sculptures. Goya
probably saw his first works of great
art there. When Goya grew up, he
painted the walls and ceilings
of some of those churches, like the
one above.

When Goya started school in his
new city, he must have shown a great
interest in art. His teachers thought

he should go to learn about art from Saragossa's master artist, José Luzán.

José Luzán taught Goya to draw by having him copy the artwork and prints of other artists. Goya also made drawings of statues that were in Saragossa. He learned other things that an artist needs to know, like how to mix colors and how to get canvas and walls ready to paint on. After spending four years with José Luzán, Goya traveled to Italy to study the great masterpieces there.

There are stories about Goya's adventures on his trip to Italy. Some of them tell of Goya fighting bulls in different towns along the way, in order to make money. No one knows if these stories are true, but his paintings show that he knew a lot about bullfighting.

Bullfights were very important to Goya throughout his life. He painted many pictures of them, and made a series of famous prints, too.

During the time Goya was learning about art, a new king started to rule Spain. King Charles III wanted to make things better for his country. He began by fixing up the capital city, Madrid. Soon it was safer to go out at night. Streets were well lighted, garbage was picked up, and new buildings and palaces were built. There were lots of empty walls in the new buildings that needed paintings and decorations. Artists from all over the world came to Madrid to help. Goya got a job there designing tapestries.

Boys Inflating a Balloon. 1778. Oil on canvas, 45¾ x 48⅞ inches.
Prado, Madrid. SuperStock

A tapestry is a beautifully woven cloth that can be hung up like a painting. They were made, during Goya's time, in factories. Workers there copied designs given to them by different artists. The painting above is one of Goya's designs.

Soon people in the royal court noticed Goya's beautiful tapestry designs and asked him to paint their pictures. He was even asked to paint a portrait of King Charles III.

One of Goya's special gifts was his ability to show not only how people looked, but also what kind of people they were in real life.

Charles III. Museo di San Martino, Naples.
Scala/Art Resources, NY

Detail of *The Family of Charles IV*. 1800–1801.
Oil on canvas, 110⅜ x 132⅜ inches.
Prado, Madrid. Bridgeman Art Library/SuperStock

Goya liked King Charles III and
painted him looking wise and
friendly. But he painted the next
king of Spain and his queen, above,
the way he knew them to be. Even
in their fancy costumes, with
jewelry and medals, Goya showed them
as dull and oafish people.

Francisco Goya loved children. The painting on the next page is one of his most famous portraits. It's fun to look at all the things Goya put in this painting. The hungry cats in the shadows give you a feeling that the boy's pet bird could be in trouble at any moment. Goya found an interesting way to sign his name, too. He put it on the card that the bird is holding in its beak. The boy's bright red suit makes him stand out from the background. But the really special thing Goya did in this portrait was to paint the boy's face so that he almost looks alive.

Don Manuel Osorio Manrique de Zuniga. Oil on canvas, 50 x 40 inches.
© 1983/88 By The Metropolitan Museum of Art, 1949.
The Jules Bache Collection

Francisco Goya was becoming one of Spain's favorite artists. He made lots of money and had friends in the royal court. Just when things seemed like they couldn't be better, something happened that changed Goya's life, and the way he painted, forever.

Detail of *The Madhouse at Zaragoza*. 1794. Oil on tin, 17⅛ x 12¾ inches.
Meadows Museum, Southern Methodist University, Dallas. Algur H. Meadows Collection

Goya became ill with a mysterious disease, and almost died. He finally got better, but the illness left him totally deaf!

Strange and frightening things began to show up in Goya's work.

He may have painted the things he felt during his illness. People were probably surprised at the new way Goya painted.

Witches' Sabbath 1797-1798. Oil on canvas, 17⅜ x 12⅛ inches.
Lazaro Galdiano Museum, Madrid. Scala/Art Resource, NY

Goya didn't put strange and frightening things in all of his work. People still asked him to do portraits and other paintings. Goya's looser, exciting brush strokes gave more movement and expression to his paintings. *The Miracle of St. Anthony* on the next page was done for the ceiling of a church. When you see it close up, it almost looks unfinished, but Goya knew that from a distance his new style would make this painting look more lifelike.

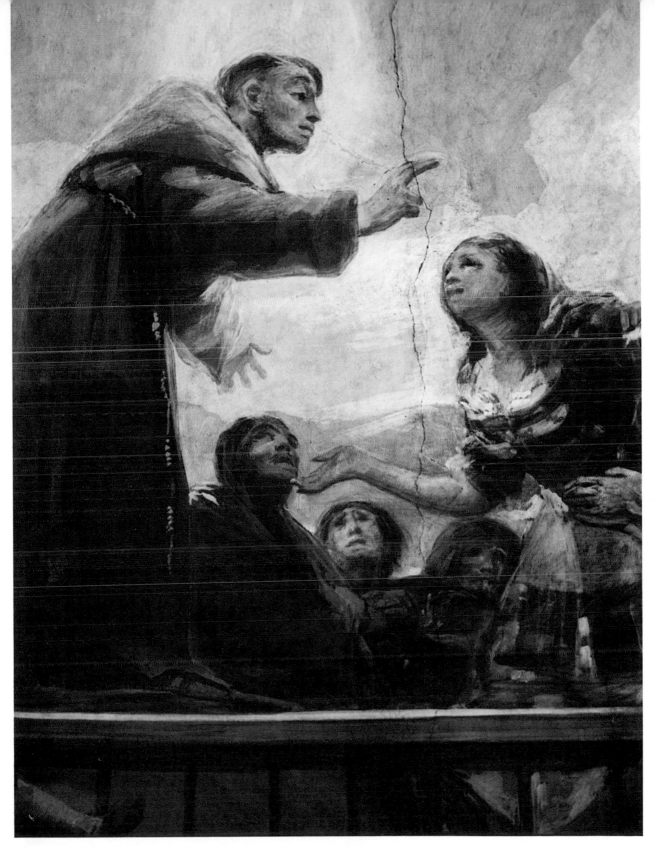

Detail of *The Miracle of St. Anthony*. 1798. 216¾ inches. Cupola fresco.
San Antonio de la Florida, Madrid. Scala/Art Resource, NY

In 1808, Goya's life changed again. Napoleon Bonaparte, a famous French general, wanted to take over Spain. Napoleon sent his soldiers there, and a bloody war began. Goya saw terrible things happening. He decided to show what he saw in his artwork.

Third Of May. c. 1814. Oil on canvas, 105 ½ x 136¾ inches. Prado, Madrid. SuperStock

Detail of the *Third of May* on page 26

The *Third of May* shows
Napoleon's soldiers shooting
defenseless Spanish people. The fear
you can see in their faces and the
strong shapes and lighting make this
one of Goya's greatest works.

When Goya was older he moved into a large house, and decided to paint the walls there. These paintings were Goya's most mysterious and powerful works. He never told anyone what they meant.

The frightening witches, strange creatures, and people fighting could have had something to do with the way Goya felt about his sickness, his deafness, the war he hated, and his old age.

Above: Detail of *Saturn Devouring One of His Children*. c. 1820-1823. Oil on gesso, 57 ½ x 32⅝ inches. Prado, Madrid. SuperStock

Left: Detail of *Two Old People Eating*. c. 1821-1823. Oil on gesso, 20⅞ x 33½ inches. Prado, Madrid. Scala/Art Resource, NY

The Fight With Cudgels. c. 1820-1821. Oil on gesso, 48½ x 104⅞ inches. Prado, Madrid. Giraudon/Art Resource, NY

Francisco Goya lived to be 82 years old. He was able to show the real deep-down feelings of the people he painted in his lifelike portraits.

Detail of child from *The Family of the Duke of Osuna* on page 4

Goya is also famous for the wonderful drawings and prints that he made. Many of them are as hard to figure out as his mysterious paintings.

Tu que no puedes (They can't help it).
Etching and burnished lithograph,
8⅖ x 5 9/10 inches. (plate).
Clarence Buckingham Collection, 1948.
Photograph © 1990, The Art Institute of Chicago.
All Rights Reserved.

Goya painted many different subjects during his life. His beautiful portraits of Spanish life are as interesting as the strange, powerful works he made after his illness.

Detail of *The Meadow at San Isidro.*
1788. Oil on canvas, 17⅜ x 37 inches.
Prado, Madrid. Scala/Art Resource, NY

Modern artists who came after Goya learned much from his exciting and expressive style of painting.

Detail of *Witches' Sabbath.*
c. 1821-23. Prado, Madrid.
Bridgeman Art Library/SuperStock

If you get a chance to see a real Goya painting, expecially the ones he did when he was older, look closely. You can see that Goya did not always paint with brushes. He often used small sticks, or reeds, to slash on paint to get the exciting feeling his paintings are known for.

The paintings in this book are in the museums listed below.

The Art Institute of Chicago
Basilica del Pilar, Zaragoza, Spain
Lazaro Galdiano Museum, Madrid, Spain
Meadows Museum, Southern Methodist University, Dallas, Texas
The Metropolitan Museum of Art, New York
Museo di San Martino, Naples, Italy
Prado, Madrid, Spain
San Antonio de la Florida (church), Madrid, Spain

LEARN MORE BY TAKING THE GOYA QUIZ!

(ANSWERS ON THE NEXT PAGE.)

1. While growing up, Francisco Goya learned to appreciate art from his father, who was a gilder. What is a gilder?

   a. Someone who prepares a canvas or wall surface for an artist before they begin their painting.

   b. A craftsman who decorates the surface of an object with a coating of gold.

   c. A worker who cleans statues, paintings, and decorative art objects that are displayed way up high in churches.

2. Goya was so busy at times that he had to work late into the night. Since there were no electric lights at the time, how was he able to see what he was painting?

   a. He kept thousands of fireflies in a cage next to his canvas.

   b. He dragged his easel and canvas outdoors whenever there was a full moon.

   c. He set candles around the brim of his hat so he could see his paintings clearly.

3. Goya was well known for the drawings he made for tapestry workers to follow. What is a tapestry?

   a. A person who taps out Morse code messages on a telegraph keypad.

   b. A musical performance where all the actors tap dance.

   c. A woven image made with colored wool or silk thread.

4. TRUE OR FALSE: Goya made lots of weird and frightening paintings to advertise a Halloween costume supply store in which he was part owner.

ANSWERS

1. **b** Francisco's father was a craftsman who coated decorative objects with a thin layer of gold. While growing up, Francisco saw lots of beautifully crafted candlesticks, picture frames, statues, and other art objects in his father's workshop. He probably met some of the artists who created them, too.

2. **c** Francisco made at least one painting where he used candles on the brim of his hat to help him see. A famous self portrait shows Goya with candle holders on his hat. If his Mom knew about this, she definitely wouldn't have approved.

3. **c** Tapestries are beautiful scenes woven on a device called a loom. In Goya's time, most tapestries were hung on the walls of royal palaces. Some of them were as large as thirteen feet wide! At a distance, a well-done tapestry can look like a painted picture.

4. **FALSE** During Goya's time paintings that showed scenes of witchcraft, sorcery, and goblins were in great demand. They were as popular then as scary horror movies are today. Goya was happy to please his clients with the weirdest pictures he could come up with—the creepier the better!